THIS MEAL PLANNER BELONGS TO:

_____

_____

_____

_____

_____

PRODUCE

DIARY

PRODUCE

CANNED GOODS

BAKERY

BEVERAGES

MEAT/DELI

FRIDGE/FREEZER

SNACKS

SEASONING

CONDIMENTS

NOTES

WEEK OF: _____

BUDGET: _____ SPENT: _____

	BREAKFAST	LUNCH	DINNER
S			
M			
T			
W			
T			
F			
S			

PRODUCE

_____
_____
_____
_____
_____
_____
_____

CANNED GOODS

_____
_____
_____
_____
_____
_____
_____

MEAT/DELI

_____
_____
_____
_____
_____
_____

SEASONING

_____
_____
_____

DIARY

_____
_____
_____
_____
_____
_____

BAKERY

_____
_____
_____
_____
_____
_____

FRIDGE/FREEZER

_____
_____
_____
_____
_____
_____

CONDIMENTS

_____
_____
_____

PRODUCE

_____
_____
_____
_____
_____
_____

BEVERAGES

_____
_____
_____
_____
_____

SNACKS

_____
_____
_____

NOTES

WEEK OF: _____

BUDGET: _____ SPENT: _____

	BREAKFAST	LUNCH	DINNER
S			
M			
T			
W			
T			
F			
S			

PRODUCE

_____
_____
_____
_____
_____
_____
_____

CANNED GOODS

_____
_____
_____
_____
_____
_____

MEAT/DELI

_____
_____
_____
_____
_____
_____

SEASONING

_____
_____
_____

DIARY

_____
_____
_____
_____
_____
_____
_____

BAKERY

_____
_____
_____
_____
_____

FRIDGE/FREEZER

_____
_____
_____
_____
_____
_____

CONDIMENTS

_____
_____
_____

PRODUCE

_____
_____
_____
_____
_____

BEVERAGES

_____
_____
_____
_____
_____

SNACKS

_____
_____
_____

NOTES

WEEK OF: _____

BUDGET: _____ SPENT: _____

	BREAKFAST	LUNCH	DINNER
S			
M			
T			
W			
T			
F			
S			

PRODUCE

DIARY

PRODUCE

CANNED GOODS

BAKERY

BEVERAGES

MEAT/DELI

FRIDGE/FREEZER

SNACKS

NOTES

SEASONING

CONDIMENTS

WEEK OF: _____

BUDGET: _____ SPENT: _____

	BREAKFAST	LUNCH	DINNER
S			
M			
T			
W			
T			
F			
S			

PRODUCE

_____
_____
_____
_____
_____
_____
_____
_____

CANNED GOODS

_____
_____
_____
_____
_____
_____
_____

MEAT/DELI

_____
_____
_____
_____
_____
_____

SEASONING

_____
_____
_____

DIARY

_____
_____
_____
_____
_____
_____
_____

BAKERY

_____
_____
_____
_____
_____
_____

FRIDGE/FREEZER

_____
_____
_____
_____
_____
_____

CONDIMENTS

_____
_____
_____

PRODUCE

_____
_____
_____
_____
_____
_____

BEVERAGES

_____
_____
_____
_____
_____
_____

SNACKS

_____
_____
_____

NOTES

WEEK OF: _____

BUDGET: _____ SPENT: _____

	BREAKFAST	LUNCH	DINNER
S			
M			
T			
W			
T			
F			
S			

PRODUCE

DIARY

PRODUCE

CANNED GOODS

BAKERY

BEVERAGES

MEAT/DELI

FRIDGE/FREEZER

SNACKS

SEASONING

CONDIMENTS

NOTES

WEEK OF: _____

BUDGET: _____ SPENT: _____

	BREAKFAST	LUNCH	DINNER
S			
M			
T			
W			
T			
F			
S			

PRODUCE	DIARY	PRODUCE
CANNED GOODS	BAKERY	BEVERAGES
MEAT/DELI	FRIDGE/FREEZER	SNACKS
SEASONING	CONDIMENTS	NOTES

WEEK OF: _____

BUDGET: _____ SPENT: _____

	BREAKFAST	LUNCH	DINNER
S			
M			
T			
W			
T			
F			
S			

PRODUCE	DIARY	PRODUCE
_____	_____	_____
_____	_____	_____
_____	_____	_____
_____	_____	_____
_____	_____	_____
_____	_____	_____
_____	_____	**BEVERAGES**
CANNED GOODS	**BAKERY**	_____
_____	_____	_____
_____	_____	_____
_____	_____	_____
_____	_____	_____
_____	_____	_____
_____	**FRIDGE/FREEZER**	**SNACKS**
_____	_____	_____
MEAT/DELI	_____	_____
_____	_____	_____
_____	_____	**NOTES**
_____	_____	
_____	**CONDIMENTS**	
SEASONING	_____	
_____	_____	
_____	_____	

WEEK OF: _____

BUDGET: _____ SPENT: _____

	BREAKFAST	LUNCH	DINNER
S			
M			
T			
W			
T			
F			
S			

PRODUCE

_____
_____
_____
_____
_____
_____
_____

CANNED GOODS

_____
_____
_____
_____
_____
_____
_____

MEAT/DELI

_____
_____
_____
_____
_____
_____

SEASONING

_____
_____
_____

DIARY

_____
_____
_____
_____
_____
_____

BAKERY

_____
_____
_____
_____
_____
_____

FRIDGE/FREEZER

_____
_____
_____
_____
_____
_____

CONDIMENTS

_____
_____
_____

PRODUCE

_____
_____
_____
_____
_____
_____

BEVERAGES

_____
_____
_____
_____
_____
_____

SNACKS

_____
_____
_____
_____

NOTES

WEEK OF: _____

BUDGET: _____ SPENT: _____

	BREAKFAST	LUNCH	DINNER
S			
M			
T			
W			
T			
F			
S			

PRODUCE	DIARY	PRODUCE

CANNED GOODS

BAKERY

BEVERAGES

FRIDGE/FREEZER

SNACKS

MEAT/DELI

CONDIMENTS

SEASONING

NOTES

WEEK OF: _____

BUDGET: _____ SPENT: _____

	BREAKFAST	LUNCH	DINNER
S			
M			
T			
W			
T			
F			
S			

PRODUCE

CANNED GOODS

MEAT/DELI

SEASONING

DIARY

BAKERY

FRIDGE/FREEZER

CONDIMENTS

PRODUCE

BEVERAGES

SNACKS

NOTES

WEEK OF: _____

BUDGET: _____ SPENT: _____

	BREAKFAST	LUNCH	DINNER
S			
M			
T			
W			
T			
F			
S			

PRODUCE	DIARY	PRODUCE

PRODUCE — DIARY — PRODUCE

CANNED GOODS

BAKERY

BEVERAGES

FRIDGE/FREEZER

SNACKS

MEAT/DELI

CONDIMENTS

NOTES

SEASONING

WEEK OF: _____

BUDGET: _____ SPENT: _____

	BREAKFAST	LUNCH	DINNER
S			
M			
T			
W			
T			
F			
S			

PRODUCE

_____
_____
_____
_____
_____
_____
_____

CANNED GOODS

_____
_____
_____
_____
_____
_____

MEAT/DELI

_____
_____
_____
_____
_____

SEASONING

_____
_____
_____

DIARY

_____
_____
_____
_____
_____

BAKERY

_____
_____
_____
_____

FRIDGE/FREEZER

_____
_____
_____
_____
_____

CONDIMENTS

_____
_____
_____

PRODUCE

_____
_____
_____
_____
_____
_____

BEVERAGES

_____
_____
_____
_____
_____

SNACKS

_____
_____

NOTES

WEEK OF: _____

BUDGET: _____ SPENT: _____

	BREAKFAST	LUNCH	DINNER
S			
M			
T			
W			
T			
F			
S			

PRODUCE	DIARY	PRODUCE
_____	_____	_____
_____	_____	_____
_____	_____	_____
_____	_____	_____
_____	_____	_____
_____	_____	_____
_____	_____	**BEVERAGES**
_____	**BAKERY**	_____
CANNED GOODS	_____	_____
_____	_____	_____
_____	_____	_____
_____	_____	_____
_____	_____	_____
_____	**FRIDGE/FREEZER**	**SNACKS**
_____	_____	_____
MEAT/DELI	_____	_____
_____	_____	_____
_____	_____	**NOTES**
_____	_____	
_____	_____	
_____	**CONDIMENTS**	
SEASONING	_____	
_____	_____	
_____	_____	

WEEK OF: _____

BUDGET: _____ SPENT: _____

	BREAKFAST	LUNCH	DINNER
S			
M			
T			
W			
T			
F			
S			

PRODUCE

_____
_____
_____
_____
_____
_____

CANNED GOODS

_____
_____
_____
_____
_____

MEAT/DELI

_____
_____
_____
_____

SEASONING

_____
_____

DIARY

_____
_____
_____
_____
_____

BAKERY

_____
_____
_____
_____
_____

FRIDGE/FREEZER

_____
_____
_____
_____
_____

CONDIMENTS

_____
_____

PRODUCE

_____
_____
_____
_____

BEVERAGES

_____
_____
_____
_____

SNACKS

_____
_____
_____

NOTES

WEEK OF: _____

BUDGET: _____ SPENT: _____

	BREAKFAST	LUNCH	DINNER
S			
M			
T			
W			
T			
F			
S			

PRODUCE

DIARY

PRODUCE

CANNED GOODS

BAKERY

BEVERAGES

FRIDGE/FREEZER

SNACKS

MEAT/DELI

NOTES

CONDIMENTS

SEASONING

WEEK OF: _____

BUDGET: _____ SPENT: _____

	BREAKFAST	LUNCH	DINNER
S			
M			
T			
W			
T			
F			
S			

PRODUCE

_____
_____
_____
_____
_____
_____
_____
_____

CANNED GOODS

_____
_____
_____
_____
_____
_____

MEAT/DELI

_____
_____
_____
_____
_____

SEASONING

_____
_____
_____

DIARY

_____
_____
_____
_____
_____
_____

BAKERY

_____
_____
_____
_____
_____

FRIDGE/FREEZER

_____
_____
_____
_____
_____
_____

CONDIMENTS

_____
_____
_____

PRODUCE

_____
_____
_____
_____
_____

BEVERAGES

_____
_____
_____
_____
_____

SNACKS

_____
_____
_____

NOTES

WEEK OF: _____

BUDGET: _____ SPENT: _____

	BREAKFAST	LUNCH	DINNER
S			
M			
T			
W			
T			
F			
S			

PRODUCE	DIARY	PRODUCE

CANNED GOODS

BAKERY

BEVERAGES

FRIDGE/FREEZER

SNACKS

MEAT/DELI

NOTES

CONDIMENTS

SEASONING

WEEK OF: _____

BUDGET: _____ SPENT: _____

	BREAKFAST	LUNCH	DINNER
S			
M			
T			
W			
T			
F			
S			

PRODUCE

DIARY

PRODUCE

CANNED GOODS

BAKERY

BEVERAGES

MEAT/DELI

FRIDGE/FREEZER

SNACKS

SEASONING

CONDIMENTS

NOTES

WEEK OF: _____

BUDGET: _____ SPENT: _____

	BREAKFAST	LUNCH	DINNER
S			
M			
T			
W			
T			
F			
S			

PRODUCE

DIARY

PRODUCE

CANNED GOODS

BAKERY

BEVERAGES

MEAT/DELI

FRIDGE/FREEZER

SNACKS

SEASONING

CONDIMENTS

NOTES

WEEK OF: _____

BUDGET: _____ SPENT: _____

	BREAKFAST	LUNCH	DINNER
S			
M			
T			
W			
T			
F			
S			

PRODUCE

DIARY

PRODUCE

CANNED GOODS

BAKERY

BEVERAGES

MEAT/DELI

FRIDGE/FREEZER

SNACKS

SEASONING

CONDIMENTS

NOTES

WEEK OF: _____

BUDGET: _____ SPENT: _____

	BREAKFAST	LUNCH	DINNER
S			
M			
T			
W			
T			
F			
S			

PRODUCE

_____
_____
_____
_____
_____
_____
_____
_____

CANNED GOODS

_____
_____
_____
_____
_____
_____

MEAT/DELI

_____
_____
_____
_____
_____
_____

SEASONING

_____
_____
_____

DIARY

_____
_____
_____
_____
_____
_____

BAKERY

_____
_____
_____
_____
_____

FRIDGE/FREEZER

_____
_____
_____
_____
_____
_____

CONDIMENTS

_____
_____
_____
_____

PRODUCE

_____
_____
_____
_____
_____
_____

BEVERAGES

_____
_____
_____
_____
_____

SNACKS

_____
_____

NOTES

WEEK OF: _____

BUDGET: _____ SPENT: _____

	BREAKFAST	LUNCH	DINNER
S			
M			
T			
W			
T			
F			
S			

PRODUCE

_____
_____
_____
_____
_____
_____
_____
_____

CANNED GOODS

_____
_____
_____
_____
_____

MEAT/DELI

_____
_____
_____
_____

SEASONING

_____
_____
_____

DIARY

_____
_____
_____
_____
_____
_____

BAKERY

_____
_____
_____
_____
_____
_____

FRIDGE/FREEZER

_____
_____
_____
_____
_____
_____

CONDIMENTS

_____
_____
_____

PRODUCE

_____
_____
_____
_____
_____

BEVERAGES

_____
_____
_____
_____
_____

SNACKS

_____
_____
_____

NOTES

WEEK OF: _____

BUDGET: _____ SPENT: _____

	BREAKFAST	LUNCH	DINNER
S			
M			
T			
W			
T			
F			
S			

PRODUCE

DIARY

PRODUCE

CANNED GOODS

BAKERY

BEVERAGES

MEAT/DELI

FRIDGE/FREEZER

SNACKS

SEASONING

CONDIMENTS

NOTES

WEEK OF: _____

BUDGET: _____ SPENT: _____

	BREAKFAST	LUNCH	DINNER
S			
M			
T			
W			
T			
F			
S			

PRODUCE

DIARY

PRODUCE

CANNED GOODS

BAKERY

BEVERAGES

MEAT/DELI

FRIDGE/FREEZER

SNACKS

NOTES

SEASONING

CONDIMENTS

WEEK OF: _____

BUDGET: _____ SPENT: _____

	BREAKFAST	LUNCH	DINNER
S			
M			
T			
W			
T			
F			
S			

PRODUCE

_____
_____
_____
_____
_____
_____
_____
_____

CANNED GOODS

_____
_____
_____
_____
_____
_____
_____

MEAT/DELI

_____
_____
_____
_____
_____
_____
_____

SEASONING

_____
_____
_____
_____

DIARY

_____
_____
_____
_____
_____
_____
_____

BAKERY

_____
_____
_____
_____
_____
_____
_____

FRIDGE/FREEZER

_____
_____
_____
_____
_____
_____

CONDIMENTS

_____
_____
_____
_____

PRODUCE

_____
_____
_____
_____
_____

BEVERAGES

_____
_____
_____
_____
_____
_____

SNACKS

_____
_____
_____

NOTES

WEEK OF: _____

BUDGET: _____ SPENT: _____

	BREAKFAST	LUNCH	DINNER
S			
M			
T			
W			
T			
F			
S			

PRODUCE

_____
_____
_____
_____
_____
_____
_____
_____

CANNED GOODS

_____
_____
_____
_____
_____
_____
_____

MEAT/DELI

_____
_____
_____
_____
_____

SEASONING

_____
_____
_____

DIARY

_____
_____
_____
_____
_____
_____
_____

BAKERY

_____
_____
_____
_____
_____
_____

FRIDGE/FREEZER

_____
_____
_____
_____
_____
_____

CONDIMENTS

_____
_____
_____

PRODUCE

_____
_____
_____
_____
_____

BEVERAGES

_____
_____
_____
_____
_____
_____

SNACKS

_____
_____
_____

NOTES

WEEK OF: _____

BUDGET: _____ SPENT: _____

	BREAKFAST	LUNCH	DINNER
S			
M			
T			
W			
T			
F			
S			

PRODUCE

DIARY

PRODUCE

CANNED GOODS

BAKERY

BEVERAGES

MEAT/DELI

FRIDGE/FREEZER

SNACKS

SEASONING

CONDIMENTS

NOTES

WEEK OF: _____

BUDGET: _____   SPENT: _____

	BREAKFAST	LUNCH	DINNER
S			
M			
T			
W			
T			
F			
S			

PRODUCE

_____
_____
_____
_____
_____
_____

CANNED GOODS

_____
_____
_____
_____
_____

MEAT/DELI

_____
_____
_____
_____
_____

SEASONING

_____
_____
_____

DIARY

_____
_____
_____
_____
_____

BAKERY

_____
_____
_____
_____

FRIDGE/FREEZER

_____
_____
_____
_____
_____

CONDIMENTS

_____
_____
_____

PRODUCE

_____
_____
_____
_____

BEVERAGES

_____
_____
_____
_____

SNACKS

_____
_____
_____

NOTES

WEEK OF: _____

BUDGET: _____ SPENT: _____

	BREAKFAST	LUNCH	DINNER
S			
M			
T			
W			
T			
F			
S			

PRODUCE	DIARY	PRODUCE

CANNED GOODS

BAKERY

BEVERAGES

FRIDGE/FREEZER

SNACKS

MEAT/DELI

NOTES

CONDIMENTS

SEASONING

WEEK OF: _____

BUDGET: _____ SPENT: _____

	BREAKFAST	LUNCH	DINNER
S			
M			
T			
W			
T			
F			
S			

PRODUCE

DIARY

PRODUCE

CANNED GOODS

BAKERY

BEVERAGES

FRIDGE/FREEZER

SNACKS

MEAT/DELI

NOTES

CONDIMENTS

SEASONING

WEEK OF: _____

BUDGET: _____ SPENT: _____

	BREAKFAST	LUNCH	DINNER
S			
M			
T			
W			
T			
F			
S			

PRODUCE

DIARY

PRODUCE

CANNED GOODS

BAKERY

BEVERAGES

MEAT/DELI

FRIDGE/FREEZER

SNACKS

SEASONING

CONDIMENTS

NOTES

WEEK OF: _____

BUDGET: _____ SPENT: _____

	BREAKFAST	LUNCH	DINNER
S			
M			
T			
W			
T			
F			
S			

PRODUCE

CANNED GOODS

MEAT/DELI

SEASONING

DIARY

BAKERY

FRIDGE/FREEZER

CONDIMENTS

PRODUCE

BEVERAGES

SNACKS

NOTES

WEEK OF: _____

BUDGET: _____ SPENT: _____

	BREAKFAST	LUNCH	DINNER
S			
M			
T			
W			
T			
F			
S			

PRODUCE

_____
_____
_____
_____
_____
_____
_____

CANNED GOODS

_____
_____
_____
_____
_____
_____

MEAT/DELI

_____
_____
_____
_____
_____

SEASONING

_____
_____
_____

DIARY

_____
_____
_____
_____
_____
_____

BAKERY

_____
_____
_____
_____

FRIDGE/FREEZER

_____
_____
_____
_____
_____
_____

CONDIMENTS

_____
_____
_____

PRODUCE

_____
_____
_____
_____
_____

BEVERAGES

_____
_____
_____
_____
_____

SNACKS

_____
_____
_____

NOTES

WEEK OF: _____

BUDGET: _____ SPENT: _____

	BREAKFAST	LUNCH	DINNER
S			
M			
T			
W			
T			
F			
S			

PRODUCE	DIARY	PRODUCE
_____	_____	_____

PRODUCE   DIARY   PRODUCE

PRODUCE

_____
_____
_____
_____
_____
_____
_____

CANNED GOODS

_____
_____
_____
_____
_____
_____

MEAT/DELI

_____
_____
_____
_____
_____

SEASONING

_____
_____
_____

DIARY

_____
_____
_____
_____
_____

BAKERY

_____
_____
_____
_____
_____

FRIDGE/FREEZER

_____
_____
_____
_____
_____
_____

CONDIMENTS

_____
_____
_____

PRODUCE

_____
_____
_____
_____
_____

BEVERAGES

_____
_____
_____
_____
_____

SNACKS

_____
_____

NOTES

WEEK OF: _____

BUDGET: _____ SPENT: _____

	BREAKFAST	LUNCH	DINNER
S			
M			
T			
W			
T			
F			
S			

PRODUCE

_____
_____
_____
_____
_____
_____
_____
_____

CANNED GOODS

_____
_____
_____
_____
_____
_____
_____

MEAT/DELI

_____
_____
_____
_____
_____

SEASONING

_____
_____
_____

DIARY

_____
_____
_____
_____
_____
_____

BAKERY

_____
_____
_____
_____
_____
_____

FRIDGE/FREEZER

_____
_____
_____
_____
_____
_____

CONDIMENTS

_____
_____
_____
_____

PRODUCE

_____
_____
_____
_____
_____

BEVERAGES

_____
_____
_____
_____
_____
_____

SNACKS

_____
_____

NOTES

WEEK OF: _____

BUDGET: _____ SPENT: _____

	BREAKFAST	LUNCH	DINNER
S			
M			
T			
W			
T			
F			
S			

PRODUCE

DIARY

PRODUCE

CANNED GOODS

BAKERY

BEVERAGES

MEAT/DELI

FRIDGE/FREEZER

SNACKS

SEASONING

CONDIMENTS

NOTES

WEEK OF: _____

BUDGET: _____ SPENT: _____

	BREAKFAST	LUNCH	DINNER
S			
M			
T			
W			
T			
F			
S			

PRODUCE

CANNED GOODS

MEAT/DELI

SEASONING

DIARY

BAKERY

FRIDGE/FREEZER

CONDIMENTS

PRODUCE

BEVERAGES

SNACKS

NOTES

WEEK OF: _____

BUDGET: _____ SPENT: _____

	BREAKFAST	LUNCH	DINNER
S			
M			
T			
W			
T			
F			
S			

PRODUCE

_____
_____
_____
_____
_____
_____
_____

CANNED GOODS

_____
_____
_____
_____
_____
_____

MEAT/DELI

_____
_____
_____
_____
_____

SEASONING

_____
_____
_____

DIARY

_____
_____
_____
_____
_____
_____

BAKERY

_____
_____
_____
_____
_____

FRIDGE/FREEZER

_____
_____
_____
_____
_____
_____

CONDIMENTS

_____
_____
_____

PRODUCE

_____
_____
_____
_____

BEVERAGES

_____
_____
_____
_____
_____

SNACKS

_____
_____
_____

NOTES

WEEK OF: _____

BUDGET: _____ SPENT: _____

	BREAKFAST	LUNCH	DINNER
S			
M			
T			
W			
T			
F			
S			

PRODUCE

_____
_____
_____
_____
_____
_____
_____
_____
_____
_____

CANNED GOODS

_____
_____
_____
_____
_____
_____
_____

MEAT/DELI

_____
_____
_____
_____
_____
_____

SEASONING

_____
_____
_____
_____

DIARY

_____
_____
_____
_____
_____
_____
_____

BAKERY

_____
_____
_____
_____
_____
_____

FRIDGE/FREEZER

_____
_____
_____
_____
_____
_____
_____

CONDIMENTS

_____
_____
_____
_____

PRODUCE

_____
_____
_____
_____
_____
_____
_____

BEVERAGES

_____
_____
_____
_____
_____
_____

SNACKS

_____
_____
_____

NOTES

WEEK OF: _____

BUDGET: _____ SPENT: _____

	BREAKFAST	LUNCH	DINNER
S			
M			
T			
W			
T			
F			
S			

PRODUCE

_____
_____
_____
_____
_____
_____
_____
_____

CANNED GOODS

_____
_____
_____
_____
_____
_____
_____

MEAT/DELI

_____
_____
_____
_____
_____
_____

SEASONING

_____
_____
_____
_____

DIARY

_____
_____
_____
_____
_____
_____

BAKERY

_____
_____
_____
_____
_____

FRIDGE/FREEZER

_____
_____
_____
_____
_____
_____
_____

CONDIMENTS

_____
_____
_____
_____
_____

PRODUCE

_____
_____
_____
_____
_____

BEVERAGES

_____
_____
_____
_____
_____
_____

SNACKS

_____
_____
_____

NOTES

WEEK OF: _____

BUDGET: _____ SPENT: _____

	BREAKFAST	LUNCH	DINNER
S			
M			
T			
W			
T			
F			
S			

PRODUCE

_____
_____
_____
_____
_____
_____
_____
_____

CANNED GOODS

_____
_____
_____
_____
_____
_____
_____

MEAT/DELI

_____
_____
_____
_____
_____
_____
_____

SEASONING

_____
_____
_____
_____

DIARY

_____
_____
_____
_____
_____
_____
_____

BAKERY

_____
_____
_____
_____
_____
_____

FRIDGE/FREEZER

_____
_____
_____
_____
_____
_____
_____

CONDIMENTS

_____
_____
_____
_____

PRODUCE

_____
_____
_____
_____
_____

BEVERAGES

_____
_____
_____
_____
_____
_____
_____

SNACKS

_____
_____
_____

NOTES

WEEK OF: _____

BUDGET: _____ SPENT: _____

	BREAKFAST	LUNCH	DINNER
S			
M			
T			
W			
T			
F			
S			

PRODUCE

_____
_____
_____
_____
_____
_____
_____

CANNED GOODS

_____
_____
_____
_____
_____
_____

MEAT/DELI

_____
_____
_____
_____
_____

SEASONING

_____
_____
_____
_____

DIARY

_____
_____
_____
_____
_____
_____

BAKERY

_____
_____
_____
_____
_____

FRIDGE/FREEZER

_____
_____
_____
_____
_____
_____

CONDIMENTS

_____
_____
_____
_____

PRODUCE

_____
_____
_____
_____
_____
_____

BEVERAGES

_____
_____
_____
_____
_____

SNACKS

_____
_____
_____

NOTES

WEEK OF: _____

BUDGET: _____ SPENT: _____

	BREAKFAST	LUNCH	DINNER
S			
M			
T			
W			
T			
F			
S			

PRODUCE

_____
_____
_____
_____
_____
_____
_____

CANNED GOODS

_____
_____
_____
_____
_____
_____

MEAT/DELI

_____
_____
_____
_____
_____

SEASONING

_____
_____
_____

DIARY

_____
_____
_____
_____
_____

BAKERY

_____
_____
_____
_____
_____

FRIDGE/FREEZER

_____
_____
_____
_____
_____
_____

CONDIMENTS

_____
_____
_____
_____

PRODUCE

_____
_____
_____
_____

BEVERAGES

_____
_____
_____
_____

SNACKS

_____
_____
_____

NOTES

WEEK OF: _____

BUDGET: _____ SPENT: _____

	BREAKFAST	LUNCH	DINNER
S			
M			
T			
W			
T			
F			
S			

PRODUCE	DIARY	PRODUCE

CANNED GOODS

BAKERY

BEVERAGES

FRIDGE/FREEZER

SNACKS

MEAT/DELI

NOTES

CONDIMENTS

SEASONING

WEEK OF: _____

BUDGET: _____ SPENT: _____

	BREAKFAST	LUNCH	DINNER
S			
M			
T			
W			
T			
F			
S			

PRODUCE

CANNED GOODS

MEAT/DELI

SEASONING

DIARY

BAKERY

FRIDGE/FREEZER

CONDIMENTS

PRODUCE

BEVERAGES

SNACKS

NOTES

WEEK OF: _____

BUDGET: _____ SPENT: _____

	BREAKFAST	LUNCH	DINNER
S			
M			
T			
W			
T			
F			
S			

PRODUCE

- _____
- _____
- _____
- _____
- _____
- _____
- _____

CANNED GOODS

- _____
- _____
- _____
- _____
- _____
- _____

MEAT/DELI

- _____
- _____
- _____
- _____
- _____

SEASONING

- _____
- _____
- _____
- _____

DIARY

- _____
- _____
- _____
- _____
- _____
- _____

BAKERY

- _____
- _____
- _____
- _____

FRIDGE/FREEZER

- _____
- _____
- _____
- _____
- _____
- _____

CONDIMENTS

- _____
- _____
- _____
- _____

PRODUCE

- _____
- _____
- _____
- _____
- _____

BEVERAGES

- _____
- _____
- _____
- _____
- _____

SNACKS

- _____
- _____
- _____

NOTES

WEEK OF: _____

BUDGET: _____ SPENT: _____

	BREAKFAST	LUNCH	DINNER
S			
M			
T			
W			
T			
F			
S			

PRODUCE

DIARY

PRODUCE

CANNED GOODS

BAKERY

BEVERAGES

MEAT/DELI

FRIDGE/FREEZER

SNACKS

SEASONING

CONDIMENTS

NOTES

WEEK OF: _____

BUDGET: _____ SPENT: _____

	BREAKFAST	LUNCH	DINNER
S			
M			
T			
W			
T			
F			
S			

PRODUCE

_____
_____
_____
_____
_____
_____
_____
_____

CANNED GOODS

_____
_____
_____
_____
_____
_____

MEAT/DELI

_____
_____
_____
_____

SEASONING

_____
_____
_____

DIARY

_____
_____
_____
_____
_____
_____

BAKERY

_____
_____
_____
_____
_____
_____

FRIDGE/FREEZER

_____
_____
_____
_____
_____
_____

CONDIMENTS

_____
_____
_____
_____

PRODUCE

_____
_____
_____
_____
_____
_____

BEVERAGES

_____
_____
_____
_____

SNACKS

_____
_____
_____

NOTES

WEEK OF: _____

BUDGET: _____ SPENT: _____

	BREAKFAST	LUNCH	DINNER
S			
M			
T			
W			
T			
F			
S			

PRODUCE

_____
_____
_____
_____
_____
_____
_____

CANNED GOODS
_____
_____
_____
_____
_____
_____

MEAT/DELI
_____
_____
_____
_____
_____

SEASONING
_____
_____
_____

DIARY

_____
_____
_____
_____
_____
_____

BAKERY
_____
_____
_____
_____
_____

FRIDGE/FREEZER
_____
_____
_____
_____
_____
_____

CONDIMENTS
_____
_____
_____
_____

PRODUCE

_____
_____
_____
_____

BEVERAGES
_____
_____
_____
_____
_____

SNACKS
_____
_____
_____
_____

NOTES

WEEK OF: _____

BUDGET: _____ SPENT: _____

	BREAKFAST	LUNCH	DINNER
S			
M			
T			
W			
T			
F			
S			

PRODUCE	DIARY	PRODUCE

PRODUCE

DIARY

PRODUCE

CANNED GOODS

BAKERY

BEVERAGES

MEAT/DELI

FRIDGE/FREEZER

SNACKS

SEASONING

CONDIMENTS

NOTES

WEEK OF: _____

BUDGET: _____ SPENT: _____

	BREAKFAST	LUNCH	DINNER
S			
M			
T			
W			
T			
F			
S			

PRODUCE	DIARY	PRODUCE

PRODUCE

_____
_____
_____
_____
_____
_____
_____
_____

CANNED GOODS

_____
_____
_____
_____
_____
_____

MEAT/DELI

_____
_____
_____
_____
_____

SEASONING

_____
_____
_____

DIARY

_____
_____
_____
_____
_____
_____
_____

BAKERY

_____
_____
_____
_____
_____

FRIDGE/FREEZER

_____
_____
_____
_____
_____
_____

CONDIMENTS

_____
_____
_____
_____

PRODUCE

_____
_____
_____
_____
_____
_____

BEVERAGES

_____
_____
_____
_____

SNACKS

_____
_____
_____

NOTES

WEEK OF: _____

BUDGET: _____ SPENT: _____

	BREAKFAST	LUNCH	DINNER
S			
M			
T			
W			
T			
F			
S			

www.ingramcontent.com/pod-product-compliance
Lightning Source LLC
Chambersburg PA
CBHW050512240426
43673CB00004B/198